ORIGAMI HOLIDAY DECORATIONS

for CHRISTMAS • HANUKKAH *and* KWANZAA

Florence Temko

Illustrations by Barbara Poeter
Based on original diagrams by Florence Temko

Photos by Dave Kutchukian

TUTTLE PUBLISHING
Boston • Rutland, Vermont • Tokyo

First published in the United States in 2003 by Tuttle Publishing, an imprint of Periplus Editions (HK) Ltd., with editorial offices at 153 Milk Street, Boston, Massachusetts 02109.

Library of Congress Cataloging-in-Publication Data

Temko, Florence.
 Origami holiday decorations for Christmas, Hanukkah, and Kwanzaa/ Florence
 Temko.—1st ed.
  p. cm
 ISBN 0-8048-3477-6 (pbk.)
  1. Origami. 2. Holiday decorations. I. Title.

TT870 .T4456 2003
736'.982—dc21   20022075060

Distributed by

North America, Latin America, and Europe
Tuttle Publishing
Distribution Center
Airport Industrial Park
364 Innovation Drive
North Clarendon, VT 05759-9436
Tel: (802) 773-8930
Fax: (802) 773-6993
Email: info@tuttlepublishing.com

Japan
Tuttle Publishing
Yaekari Building, 3F
5-4-12 Ōsaki, Shinagawa-ku
Tokyo 141-0032
Tel: 81-35-437-0171
Fax: 81-35-437-0755
Email: tuttle-sales@gol.com

Asia Pacific
Berkeley Books Pte. Ltd.
130 Joo Seng Road
#06-01/03 Olivine Building
Singapore 368357
Tel: (65) 6280-3320
Fax: (65) 6280-6290
Email: inquiries@periplus.com.sg

First edition
08 07 06 05 04 03   9 8 7 6 5 4 3 2 1

Design by Barbara Poeter, Bomoseen, Vermont
Printed in Singapore

CONTENTS

PROJECTS

◣ Introduction

Origami Holiday Decorations shows you how to brighten Christmas, Hanukkah, and Kwanzaa with paper ornaments. Origami is the craft of folding a piece of paper into a recognizable object using only your hands. Many people are fascinated with origami and find it to be a relaxing, yet challenging hobby.

Decorating Christmas trees with origami has become a tradition in many homes, libraries, and museums. Origami ornaments have also found their way into Hanukkah celebrations, but this is the first time that a book includes such ideas for Kwanzaa. Some of the projects relate to a specific holiday, but most of them make wonderful decorations for any of the three holidays.

In Origami Holiday Decorations you will find a lot of practical information, including:

- Step-by-step instructions
- How to make unique ornaments and decorations
- How to create new designs
- How to use different papers
- How to teach origami to others
- How to use origami as an educational tool
- How origami fits into the world of computers and technology

I hope you will find that it's great fun to make holiday ornaments that can produce "oohs" and "aahs" year after year.

◣ About Origami Techniques

To help you make sense of the lines and arrows on the drawings, you should study the explanations of a few basic techniques. It will be well worth a few minutes to learn to recognize the "Four Important Symbols" and "Three Procedures," which are international standards for origami.

Any action to be taken at each step is shown in red on the diagrams.

FOUR IMPORTANT SYMBOLS

Learn to recognize these four simple clues, which are often overlooked by beginners.

1. Valley Fold

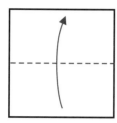

Fold the square in half by bringing one edge of the paper toward you and matching it to the opposite edge.

A valley fold is always shown by a line of dashes. You have made a valley fold.

With this one simple fold, you have made a greeting card.

2. Mountain Fold

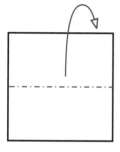

Fold the square in half by guiding one edge of the paper to the back and matching it to the opposite edge. A mountain fold is shown by a dash-dot-dash line and an arrow.

You have made a mountain fold.

With this one simple fold you have made a tent.

3. Arrows

Make a valley fold.

Double arrow — Fold and unfold.

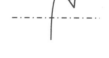

Make a mountain fold.

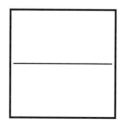

Curly arrow — Turn the paper over.

4. Existing Crease

An existing crease, made previously, is shown by a thin line that does not touch the edges.

Existing crease

THREE PROCEDURES

In these three procedures, which occur frequently in paperfolding, several steps are combined into one standard process.

1. Inside Reverse Fold

One of the most common procedures is called an inside reverse fold.

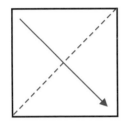 1. Fold a small square from corner to corner.

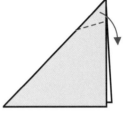 2. Place the paper exactly as shown. Fold the top corner over to the right, so that it peeks over the open edge.

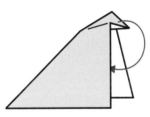 3a. Let the paper open up and push the corner in between the two layers of paper, on the creases you made in Step 2.

3b. Close up the paper.

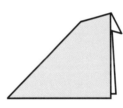 4. Completed inside reverse fold

The instructions for making an inside reverse fold are indicated with a dash-dot-dash line, the same as for a mountain fold, but the text states that you must make an inside reverse fold.

You may wonder why this procedure is called a reverse fold: In Step 2 you will see that the doubled paper is made up of a mountain fold on the front layer and a valley fold on the back layer. After you have pushed the corner in between the two layers of paper in Step 3, you have "reversed" the valley fold into a mountain fold.

2. Outside Reverse Fold

With an outside reverse fold, the paper is wrapped around the outside of a corner.

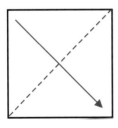 1. Fold a small square from corner to corner.

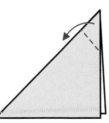 2. Place the paper exactly as shown. Valley fold the top corner over to the left, so that it peeks over the folded edge.

3a. Unfold Step 2.

3b. Let the paper open up and valley fold on the creases made in Step 2.

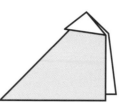

4. Completed outside reverse fold

Outside reverse folds are often used for heads, feet, and hats. The instructions for making an outside reverse fold are indicated with a dashed line, the same as for a valley fold, but the text states that you must make an outside reverse fold.

3. Rabbit's Ear

A rabbit's ear is always formed on a triangle, whenever it occurs during the folding of a model.

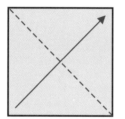

1. Fold a square from corner to corner.

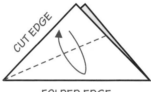

2. You now have a triangle. Fold one of the shorter cut edges to the long folded edge. Unfold it.

3. Fold the other short cut edge to the long folded edge. Unfold it.

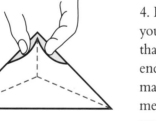

4. Pinch the corner between your thumb and forefinger so that it forms a valley fold that ends where the two creases made in Step 2 and Step 3 meet. The corner will stand up like a rabbit's ear.

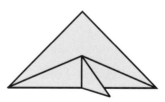

5. Completed Rabbit's Ear

HOW TO CUT PAPER SQUARES

Many of the projects in this book begin with a square piece of paper. All its sides are of equal length and all corners are right (90-degree) angles. Paper can be squared on a board paper cutter, if available, but it's quite easy to cut any rectangular sheet into a square:

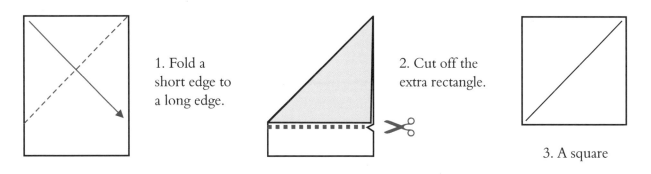

1. Fold a short edge to a long edge.

2. Cut off the extra rectangle.

3. A square

Sheets of 8 ½" x 11" copy and other printing papers can be cut into two sizes:

- With one cut: into squares with 8 ½" sides.
- With two cuts: into two squares with 5 ½" sides.

Copy shops will usually cut a whole ream for a small fee. A ream will provide five hundred 8 ½" squares or one thousand 5 ½" squares.

HELPFUL TIPS

If you are having trouble with a step check the following:

1. Make sure you distinguish carefully between a valley fold (dashed line) and a mountain fold (dash-dot-dash line).

2. Be sure to observe the curly arrow asking you to turn the paper over.

3. Compare your paper to the illustrations for:

- The step you are working on
- The previous step
- The next step, which is your goal

4. Read the directions out loud.

Drawings

For the sake of clarity, the illustrations may increase in size from the beginning of the project to the end. But the angles are always consistent, and you can test your own paper against them.

Measurements

Measurements are given in inches and centimeters, but the conversion may not always be exact in order to avoid awkward fractions. In some cases specific sizes are recommended, but in most cases you may use smaller or larger pieces of paper.

ABOUT PAPER

Most fairly thin, uncoated papers with a crisp surface are suitable for origami. Check out "origami" on the Internet for suppliers of specialty papers. Once you know how to fold an origami, you may want to reproduce it with a paper in a more appropriate color or design, which can make a big difference to the end result.

The following is an overview of the papers most popular with experienced paperfolders.

Origami Paper

Ready-cut squares in varying sizes and colors are available in some art, museum, and gift stores and from catalogs. They are usually colored on one side and white on the other. I recommend 6" (15 cm) as the most versatile all-purpose size. From there you can go on to smaller and larger squares as appropriate for a particular design.

Computer and Bond Paper; Printing Paper in Bright Colors

These types of paper are available in a large assortment of colors at copy shops, office supply stores, and school suppliers. They are sold in size 8 ½" by 11" in packages of 500 sheets (a ream), and are available in two weights, described on the packages as 24 lbs and 20 lbs. The lighter weight paper folds more easily. Printing papers are the most economical choice for schools, youth groups, and other large groups.

Gift Wrap Paper

It is quite difficult to cut paper on rolls into squares, but well worthwhile for special results. Foil gift wrap turns any origami instantly into a festive ornament.

Handmade Paper

This type of paper is softer, but gives rich-looking results. Japanese washi paper in glorious patterns is available in sheets or packages of squares.

Paper Colored on Both Sides

Some projects look better when made from paper that is colored on both sides, such as printing paper. Duo-colored origami squares, sold in packets, have different colors on the front and the back. You can make your own fancy duo papers by gluing sheets of gift wrap or other papers back to back with spray glue or glue sticks.

Recycled Paper

Out-of-date flyers, colorful magazine pages, and other discarded papers can be cut into squares and folded into origami models.

◣ ABOUT CHRISTMAS, HANUKKAH, AND KWANZAA

CHRISTMAS

Christmas was first celebrated in Europe in the fourth century on the 25th day of December to commemorate the birth of the Christ child. Since then, many symbols have become associated with the festivity.

Decorating evergreen trees with ornaments became an enduring tradition, representing long life and immortality. In the sixteenth century German people commonly decorated fir trees with flowers, fruit, and even pieces of paper. Candles were added later on to emulate the twinkling of stars.

The name of Santa Claus, the gift giver, is the abbreviation of St. Nicholas, a Turkish bishop who performed many loving acts of kindness in the fourth century and became known as the patron saint of children. His fame spread throughout Europe. In the United States he was popularized by the poem "'Twas the Night Before Christmas" written by Clement Moore in 1863 and illustrated with the now often-reproduced images by artist Thomas Nast. According to legend Santa Claus lives at the North Pole and on Christmas Eve travels on his sled drawn by reindeer to deliver gifts for boys and girls.

HANUKKAH

The Jewish Festival of Lights, called Hanukkah, is celebrated by lighting candles for eight consecutive evenings at sunset. The ceremony commemorates a miracle that happened after Jews won a battle in the year 165 B.C.

As recorded in the Book of Maccabees, two thousand years ago a Syrian king, Antiochus, governed Israel. He wanted to force the Jews to give up their belief in one God and take on the Greek religion. The Jews struggled to keep their own traditions. When their sacred temple in Jerusalem was overrun by the Syrian army, the Maccabee brothers fled and formed a fighting band, which defeated the Syrian soldiers after three years.

On their return to Jerusalem the Maccabees wanted to rededicate their temple by lighting the sacred oil lamp. According to legend they could only find a tiny bit of sacred oil, expected to last for a single day. Much to their surprise the light continued to burn for eight days. In memory of this miracle Jewish families celebrate Hanukkah every year.

KWANZAA

In the 1960s African American people began celebrating a seven-day holiday during December to honor their African heritage. They named it "Kwanzaa," a Swahili word meaning "first fruits of the harvest." Kwanzaa is now widely observed in the United States in homes, schools, churches, museums, and libraries. Because Kwanzaa is an ethnic festival, it can be celebrated side-by-side with Christmas and other religious holidays.

Each night of Kwanzaa black, red, and green candles are lighted in a seven-armed candleholder. The candles represent Nguzo Saba, the seven principles of day-to-day living, which underlie Kwanzaa. Beginning on December 25 a different principle is honored each night: Unity (*umoja* in Swahili); self-determination (*kujichagulia*); collective work and responsibility (*ujima*); cooperative economics (*ujamaa*); purpose (*nia*); creativity (*kuumba*); and faith (*imani*).

Colorful local festivals held during the week of Kwanzaa commemorate African culture and cooking, with the stress on active participation in craft workshops and frequent discussions of the meaning of Kwanzaa.

◤ FAQ *(Frequently Asked Questions)*

What is the history of paperfolding?

"Origami" is a Japanese word consisting of *ori*, meaning to fold, and *gami*, meaning paper. The word has slipped into the English language because paperfolding has spread from Japan, where it is part of the culture. It is known that since the twelfth century paper has been folded in Japan for ceremonial purposes and that in the sixteenth century paper was folded for decorative use and entertainment.

Records show that paper was folded in Europe in the fourteenth century. In the sixteenth and seventeenth centuries it was common practice to fold square baptismal certificates in set patterns.

The kind of recreational origami now popular in Asia and Western countries began in the late nineteenth century, but received its greatest impetus in the latter half of the twentieth century. Akira Yoshizawa in Japan, Lillian Oppenheimer in the United States, and Robert Harbin in England were prominent forces in bringing origami to the attention of the general public.

Is origami art or craft?

Origami is definitely a craft, with an underlying technique, but some models are well recognized as works of art. They have been displayed in major art museums and sold in art galleries.

The most prolific creators seem to have a mathematical, a scientific, or an artistic inclination of which they may not even be aware. Robert Lang and Akira Yoshizawa are two of the foremost artists.

Dr. Robert Lang, an American scientist, designed a now famous cuckoo clock, which requires about 260 intricate folds. He is intrigued by the challenge of devising insects that duplicate their natural details. He has devised the Treemaker software, which bases folding patterns on proportions of the location and size of points on the surface of the paper.

Akira Yoshizawa of Japan is considered the master of artistic origami, which are much admired. His animals seem to come alive and be poised ready to run or jump.

Why fold paper?

Many people find pleasure in the folding process itself when following the diagrams, while others can't wait to achieve the result. Still others enjoy the challenge of inventing entirely new designs and some paperfolders like to teach origami to friends, or in schools and libraries.

Is origami creative?

Paperfolders constantly create new models. Once you know some of the basics, you may begin to create your own simple toys, home decorations, or complex sculptures. They may be variations on existing models or entirely new. Some may appear in just minutes, like a doodle, while others may be so complex that they take months to design and hours to reproduce.

What are some practical uses for origami?

- Entertaining friends and strangers
- Making ornaments and decorations
- Aiding curriculum requirements in math, art, and social science classes
- Fund-raising

How long does it take to learn origami?

You can learn to make a simple model in just a few minutes, while a complex one may be a challenge for many hours. The models in this book vary from simple to intermediate. The more you fold paper, the easier it becomes, in a remarkably short period of time.

At what age can children learn origami?

I have taught three-year-olds on a one-on-one basis, but generally the necessary coordination begins to develop at seven years of age.

How can I teach others?

It's one thing to teach one-on-one in an informal setting and quite another to give a program to a class or other group. In my general introductory programs, I teach groups to make a gift box, a swan, and a leaping frog. I may vary this, depending on special requests by the organizers or the seasons of the year. Before any presentation:

- Decide clearly what you would like to teach.
- Make sure you know how to fold the models, making them over and over until you are familiar with them, verbalizing each step to yourself.
- Prepare the quantity and types of papers you will need, including larger squares for demonstrating up front.

What is the best way to make sharp creases?

Fold the paper on a tabletop or other solid surface. This provides resistance and helps you make straight creases. You can sharpen the creases with your fingernail or an ice-cream stick.

What are the best sizes for models?

Paperfolders call a completed origami a model. Origami models can be made in any size, depending on your own preference. When you make a model for the first time it is best to use a square between 6" to 10" (15 cm to 25 cm). Then you may decide to make the model smaller or larger by using a smaller or larger square to suit the purpose.

What are bases?

Many models begin with the same series of steps, which are called bases. They are recognized by paperfolders all over the world. In ***Origami Holiday Decorations*** bases occur in the following models:

- *Kite base:* Icicle, Snowflake Card, Christmas Tree, Turkey
- *Blintz base:* Hanging Ornament, Holiday Wreath, Picture Frame, Kwanzaa Bowl
- *Fish base:* Dove Candy Dish
- *Triangle base:* Santa Claus
- *Square or Preliminary base:* Star of Bethlehem, Reindeer
- *Bird base:* Star of Bethlehem or Reindeer

What is origami language?

When paperfolders show each other new models they may say: "Begin with the Kite base." The other person will know what to do. These and other terms like valley fold, mountain fold, and so on are shortcuts that keep recurring in origami instructions. In **Origami Holiday Decorations** I have referred to them as "origami language."

If we accept one dictionary definition of the word "language" as "any mode of communication," then origami itself is a language. When paperfolders find themselves in situations where they have no common language with other people, they often fold and give away an origami bird or toy. They are communicating very well, eliciting smiles and friendship.

Where do models originate?

There are three sources:

- *Traditional:* In many cultures toys are folded from paper, like the dart airplane or the hat made from a newspaper.
- *Known creators:* When paperfolders show or teach models by known creators, they always credit them by name.
- *Unknown creators:* When a model is handed around informally at parties, in schools, and elsewhere, the name of the creator may become lost in the shuffle.

What about copyrights?

You may fold any origami and photocopy printed instructions for your own personal use. You cannot include them in handouts or any printed or electronic format without permission from the creator or copyright holder, which may be a publisher. For more detailed information consult the guidelines provided by OrigamiUSA (see the address at the end of this chapter).

How can I meet other paperfolders?

It's great fun to meet with other paperfolders. Origami clubs where members of all ages meet monthly to exchange directions for models and share other information exist in many localities. OrigamiUSA holds an annual convention in New York City attended by more than 600 enthusiasts from many countries. Other conventions take place in different places. Origami is well represented on the Internet, which can satisfy your curiosity about any of its aspects. Traditional and new designs, whether simple or complex, appear constantly on web sites.

Further Information

Readers interested in learning more about paperfolding can use the keyword "origami" on the Internet. These American and British groups can connect you with other paperfolders in your area or your country:

OrigamiUSA
15 West 77th Street
New York, NY 10024
USA

British Origami Society
2A The Chestnuts
Countesthorpe, Leicester
LE8 5TL, United Kingdom

◣ ICICLE

Origami icicles can add sparkle to any tree. Decorate a whole tree with silver icicles, or choose a riot of bright shades of red, gold, and green. The secret lies in using shiny foil gift wrap. Small icicles can fill in the annoying holes that always seem to develop when decorating a Christmas tree.

You need:

A 3″ (7 cm) square of foil gift wrap

If paper is colored on only one side, begin with the white side up.

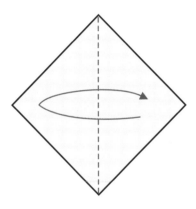

1a. Fold the square from corner to corner.

1b. Unfold it.

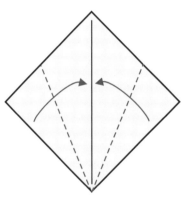

2. Fold two edges to the crease you just made.

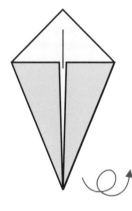

3. Turn the paper over. In origami language, this shape is called a Kite base.

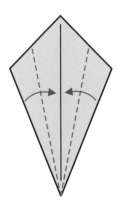

4. Fold the two long edges to the middle.

5. Reach behind for the corners of the paper. Bring them out to the sides.

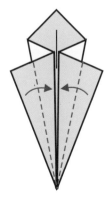

6. Fold the sides to the middle.

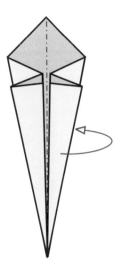
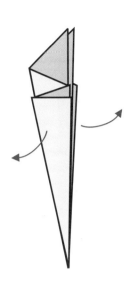

7. Mountain fold the Icicle in half to the back.

8. Loosen the pleats.

9. Completed Icicle

◣ SNOWFLAKE CARD

For a very effective greeting card fold six icicles from plain white printing paper, or select a paper with flecks or texture.

You need:

> *Six 2″ (5 cm) squares of white paper*
>
> *A piece of construction or handmade paper*
>
> *Glue*

If paper is colored on one side only, begin with the colored side facing up.

Fold all six squares in the same way.

   1a. Fold the paper as in Steps 1 through 5 of the Icicle.

   1b. Turn the paper over.

   1c. Fold the construction paper in half.

   1d. Glue the icicles in a circle on the construction paper.

Holiday Party

Making snowflake cards lends itself well to a group activity, whether it be a family, a class, or a youth workshop.

◣ SANTA'S HAT DECORATION

Santa's Hat can be used as unusual place cards for Christmas dinner or their jaunty lines can add a spot of color anywhere in the house. You could put one on a Teddy Bear's head for a seasonal touch.

You need:

A paper square, red on one side and white on the other

Begin with the colored side of the paper facing up.

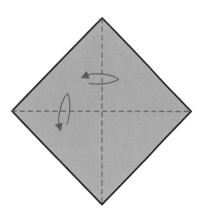

1a. Fold the square from corner to corner in both directions.

1b. Unfold the paper each time.

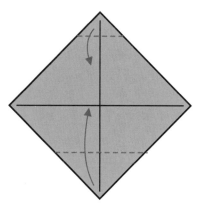

2a. Fold the top corner down a little.

2b. Fold the bottom corner to the crease that goes across the center of the paper.

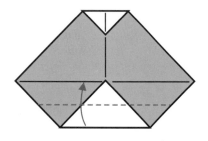

3. Fold the bottom edge to the crease that goes across the center of the paper.

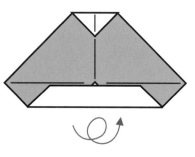

4. Turn the paper over.

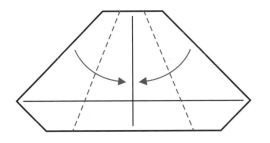

5. Fold the slanted edges to the middle crease.

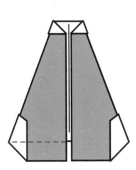

6. On the left, fold the bottom edge up.

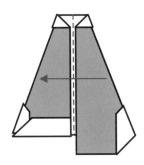

7. Fold the hat in half.

8a. With a mountain fold, push the bottom edge into the pocket formed by two layers of paper. This locks the hat together.

8b. Twist the top of the hat at an angle.

9. Completed Santa's Hat. To make the hat stand up spread the bottom apart.

Santa's Elves

You can make an Elf Finger Puppet when you fold Santa's Hat from a 4" (10 cm) paper square. Children can make several puppets and hold a conversation between them. Perhaps they can talk about what gifts they would like to receive.

ZAWADI GIFT (MESSAGE RACK)

An origami message rack would be a possible Kwanzaa gift. Although spiritual values are emphasized during the festival, gifts called Zawadi (zah-WAH-dee), are exchanged. They are often handmade or educational in keeping with the principle of kuumba (koo-OOM-ba), which means creativity. Messages can be deposited in the pockets of the rack.

You need:

A piece of paper, 8 ½" x 11" (or A4)

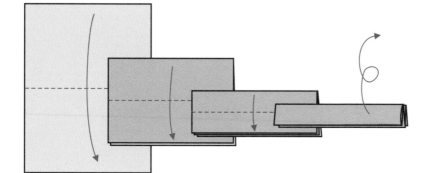

1a. Fold the paper in half the short way.

1b. Fold in half again.

1c. Fold in half a third time.

1d. Unfold the paper so that it lies flat.

2a. Place the colored side of the paper face up. Number the seven creases.

2b. Valley fold crease 2 and mountain fold crease 3.

2c. Valley fold crease 5 and mountain fold crease 6.

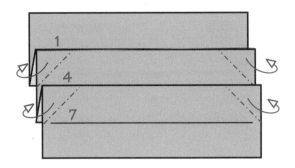

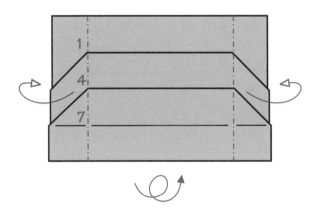

3. Mountain fold the four corners under, as shown.

4a. Mountain fold the long edges to the back.

4b. Turn the paper over.

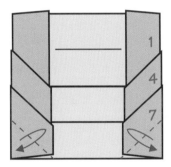

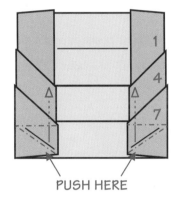

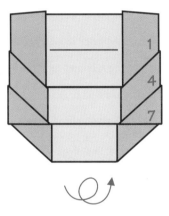

5a. Fold in the two bottom corners.

5b. Unfold them.

6. Lock the paper by pushing the corners under the folded edge. See the next illustration.

PUSH HERE

7. Back of the Message Rack. Turn it over.

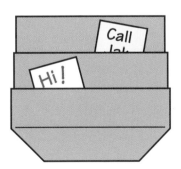

8. Completed Message Rack

Large Message Rack with Many Pockets

By starting with a larger piece of paper you can make a Message Rack with more pockets to keep messages for everyone in the family. Almost any large rectangle will do; I have made a very practical one for my family from a piece of gift wrap 10" x 20" (25 cm x 50 cm) with four pockets. In the lower pocket we keep scratch paper and attach a pen for writing messages.

In order to make a larger Message Rack, in Step 1, fold the paper in half four times, instead of three times.

HOLIDAY CALENDAR

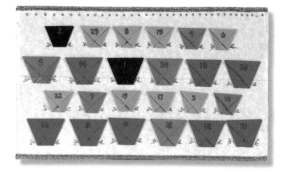

A Holiday Calendar helps contain children's impatient excitement by counting down every day in December before Kwanzaa, Hanukkah, or Christmas. For each day the calendar displays a pocket, which is glued on foamboard or cardboard. Children open one of the pockets each day to find an origami as a hidden surprise.

For Christmas make a calendar with 24 pockets. For Kwanzaa, which begins on December 26, make a total of 25 pockets. For Hanukkah, which does not always fall on the same day in the month of December, make as many pockets as are needed.

Preparing Holiday Calendars as gifts is a good family, classroom, or youth group project.

You need:

> *12 paper squares with 5 ½″ (15 cm) sides, in one color*
>
> *12 paper squares with 4 ¼″ (7 cm) sides, in another color*
>
> *Foamboard or strong cardboard 22″ x 14″ (55 cm x 35 cm)*
>
> *Glue*
>
> *Double-sided tape*

If the paper is colored on only one side, begin with the white side facing up.

HOW TO MAKE THE POCKETS

Fold all of the squares in the same way.

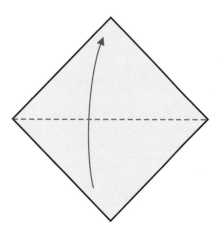

1. Fold a square from corner to corner.

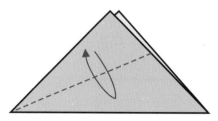

2a. Fold a short edge of the triangle to the long edge.

2b. Unfold it.

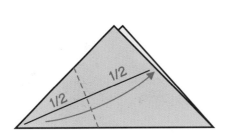

3. Fold the crease you have just made in half.

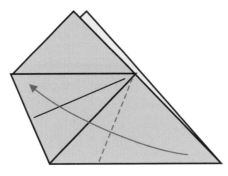

4. Fold the other corner over.

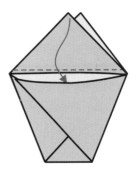

5. Fold down a single layer of the top corner and push it into the pocket made in the previous step.

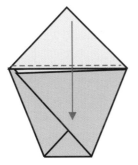

6. Fold the top corner down.

7. Completed Pocket

HOW TO ASSEMBLE THE CALENDAR

1a. Glue all pockets onto the foam-board in a regular pattern or at random. It is best to put a blob of glue in the middle of the pocket rather than glue down the whole back. This allows more room in the pocket for the surprise.

1b. Write the number for the day on which each pocket is to be opened.

2. Open each pocket by lifting up the single layer of paper, and insert the origami gift. Then seal it shut with double-sided tape.

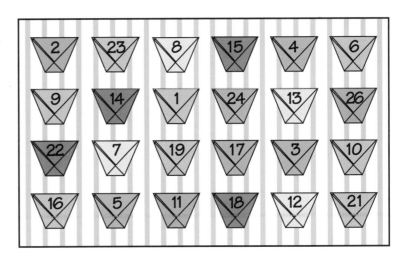

◣ HANGING ORNAMENT

This design is very easy to make but extremely versatile. A single ornament can be used as a star, three in varying sizes can be strung together as a mobile, or many of them can be scattered to stand on the dinner table.

Glittery foil paper gives the best effect. I usually glue two squares of foil gift wrap back to back for a two-tone effect.

You need:

A 3″ (8 cm) square of double-faced foil paper, or larger

Begin with the stronger color of the paper facing up.

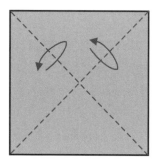

1a. Fold a square from corner to corner, in both directions.

1b. Unfold it both times.

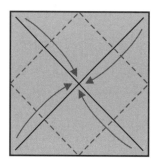

2. Fold the four corners to the center.

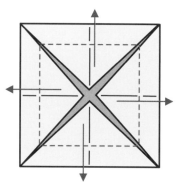

3. Fold each of the four corners from the middle out, past the outside edge.

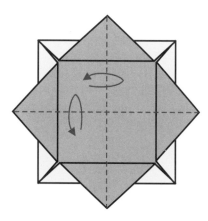

4. Valley fold the paper in half in both directions. Unfold it both times. These creases begin and end at corners, which are the corners of the original square. Unfold it.

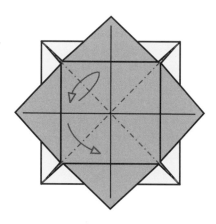

5. Make two mountain folds to the back, as shown. Unfold only the first one.

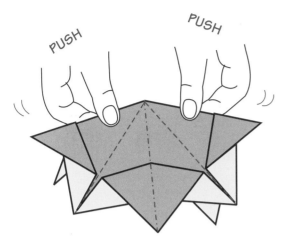

6. Push the paper into three dimensions on the mountain and valley folds made in Steps 4 and 5.

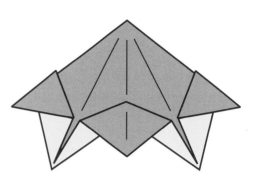

7. Completed Hanging Ornament

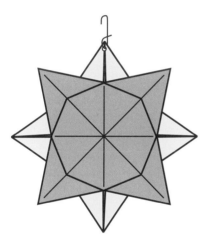

STAR

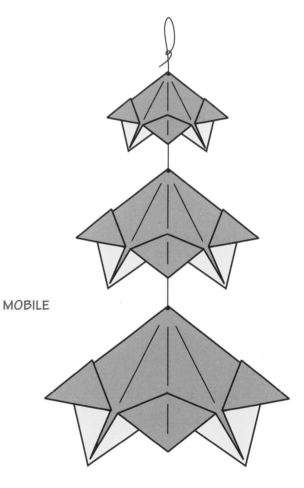

MOBILE

Star

Suspend the ornament from a corner.

Mobile

Make three ornaments from 3", 4 ½", and 6" (8 cm, 11 cm, and 14 cm) squares. String them together in a row, through the center of the ornaments. Knot a small button under each ornament to keep it from slipping.

◤ DREIDEL

During the eight-day-long Hanukkah celebration, Jewish children like to play a game with a spinning top, called a dreidel. Its four sides are decorated with Hebrew letters.

You can make origami dreidel decorations from paper squares. They can be hung around the home or school, or made into gifts of necklaces for members of your family and friends.

You need:

A paper square

If paper is colored on only one side, begin with the white side facing up.

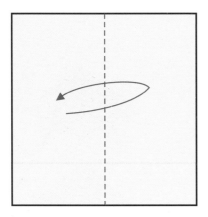

1a. Fold the square in half.

1b. Unfold it.

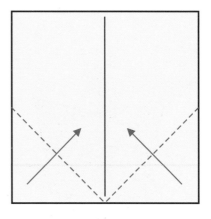

2. Fold two corners to the crease you just made.

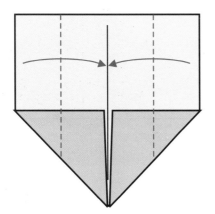

3. Fold both sides to the middle crease.

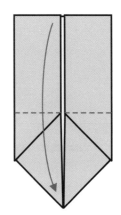

4. Fold the top edge to the bottom corner.

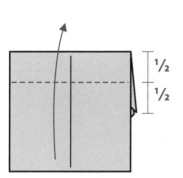

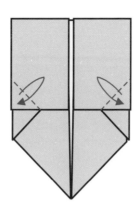

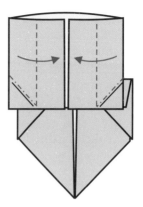

5. Fold the paper up again, making a pleat.

6a. Fold the corners in, as shown.

6b. Unfold them.

7. Fold the outside edges to the middle. As you do this, let the small triangles spread open on the creases made in Step 6. See the next drawing. Sharpen all creases.

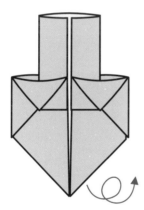

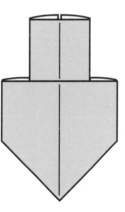

8. Turn the paper over.

9. Completed Dreidel

The Hebrew Letters

The four Hebrew letters shown on the four dreidels in the garland are: *nun, gimmel, heh,* and *shin.* They represent the words *nes godal haya sham,* which translates into "A great miracle happened there." This refers to the story of the Maccabees, which is celebrated on Hanukkah.

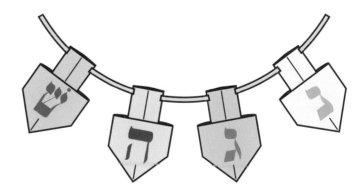

◣ THE THREE KINGS

At Christmas time you can make an origami display of the Three Kings from the East. They followed a bright star in the evening sky, which led them to the manger, where they worshiped Baby Jesus. They arrived twelve days after his birth, bearing gifts of gold, frankincense, and myrrh. (Frankincense and myrrh are resins extracted from gum trees for producing incense and perfumes, which were rare and highly valued.) In remembrance of this event the Festival of The Three Kings, also called the Epiphany, is celebrated on January 6th.

You need:

> *Three squares of origami paper in three different bright colors or gift wrap with small patterns, with sides between 6˝ and 10"*
> *(15 cm and 25 cm)*
>
> *Scraps of pink or brown paper and scraps of gold foil paper*
>
> *Scissors*
>
> *Glue*

Fold all Three Kings in the same way. Begin with the colored side of the paper facing up.

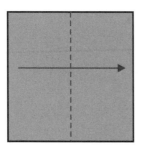
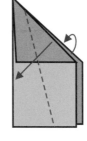
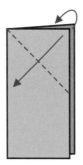

1. Fold the square in half.

2. Fold the top corner to the folded edge, first on the front, then on the back.

3. Fold the side over at an angle, first on the front, then on the back.

4a. Fold out the bottom corners of the robe to make a stand.

4b. Loosen the paper to let the figure stand.

5. Cut a face from pink or brown paper and a crown from gold paper. Glue them to the top of the robe.

6. Completed Three Kings

◣ CHRISTMAS TREE

You can make your own Christmas cards by pasting a tree to the front of a folded piece of stationery or handmade paper. Or paste three trees in different sizes on a gift package for a special effect.

You need:

A square of green paper

If paper is colored on only one side, begin with white side of paper facing up.

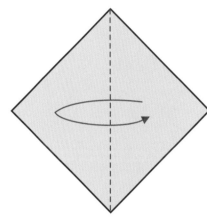

1. Fold the square from corner to corner. Unfold it.

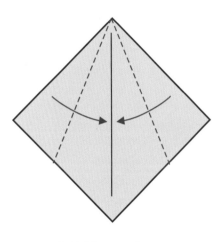

2. Fold two edges to the crease.

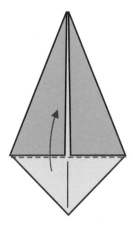

3. In origami language this shape is called a Kite base. Fold up the bottom triangle.

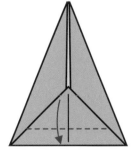

4. Fold the corner down, making a pleat.

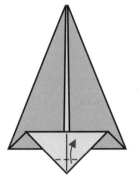

5. Fold the tip of the corner up.

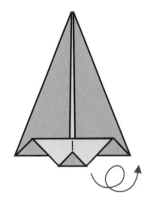

6. Turn the paper over.

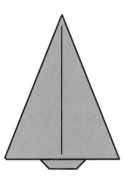

7. Completed Christmas Tree

◣ FESTIVE NAPKIN

Much care is usually taken to set a beautiful table for holiday meals. You can add a festive touch by folding napkins into butterflies. Place a folded napkin next to each setting, or put it in a glass when it will add height without crowding the space on the tabletop.

The folding pattern works well for paper or cloth napkins, even if they are not exactly square.

You need:

A napkin

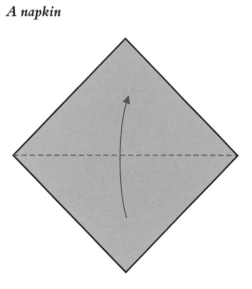

1. Fold the napkin from corner to corner.

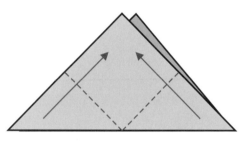

2. Fold the two outside corners to the top corner.

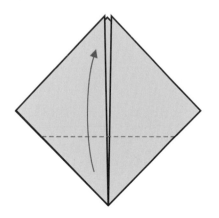

3. Fold the bottom corner up, but not all the way to the top.

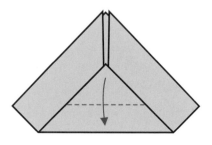

4. Fold the same corner down to the bottom edge.

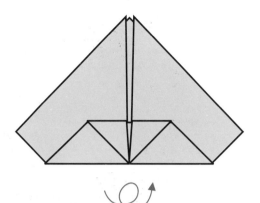

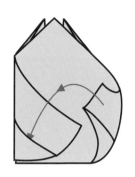

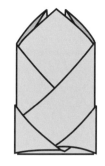

5. Turn the napkin over from front to back.

6. Tuck the right side into the left side, leaving the napkin rounded.

7. Turn the napkin around.

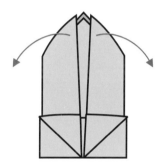

8. Pull the top corners to the outside.

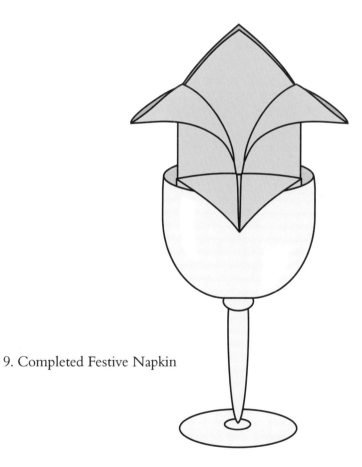

9. Completed Festive Napkin

◤ HOLIDAY WREATH

Many children know how to make a Fortune Teller from a piece of notebook paper. Here, six of these popular toys are combined into a Holiday Wreath, suitable for Christmas, Hanukkah, and Kwanzaa decorating.

The finished wreath has an interesting interdenominational feature. It is obviously a Christmas wreath, but the inside rim forms a six-pointed star, suitable for a Jewish Hanukkah decoration. For a Kwanzaa wreath, use two pieces of construction paper in red, two in black, and two in green.

It is best to use paper that is colored on both sides.

You need:

> **6 paper squares**
>
> **Glue**

Fold all six squares in the same way.

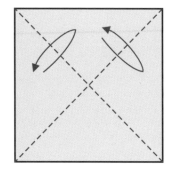

1a. Fold a square from corner to corner, in both directions.

1b. Unfold it both times.

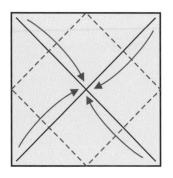

2. Fold the four corners to the center.

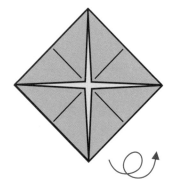

3. In origami language this shape is called a Blintz base. Turn the paper over from front to back.

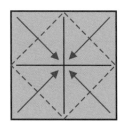

4. Fold the four corners to the center again.

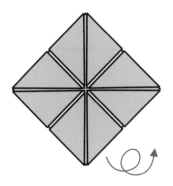

5. Turn the paper over.

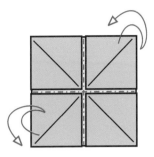

6. Mountain fold the paper to the back both ways, unfolding them both times.

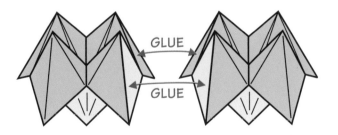

7. Slide your thumbs and forefingers into the square pockets, as shown, and press your hands toward each other.

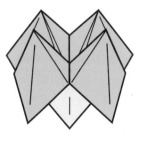

8. You have now made a classic Fortune Teller.

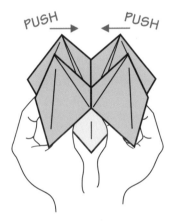

9a. When you have folded all six squares, glue the sides of two Fortune Tellers together. Each side is made up of two triangles.

9b. Glue all six Fortune Tellers in a row. Then form a circle and glue the two ends together. Tip: Hold the units together with paper clips while the glue is drying.

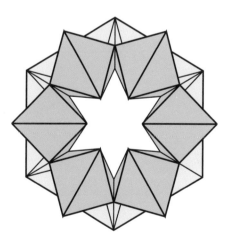

10. Completed Holiday Wreath

MONEY FLOWER

You can make a very attractive gift of money by folding two bills of any denomination into a flower. The folded bills enclose two Hershey's Kisses for a stamen and are attached to a stem of floral wire. Of all the origami models I give away, this is one of the most popular.

You need:

> *2 dollar bills*
>
> *A grocery store twist tie*
>
> *A toothpick*
>
> *2 Hershey's Kisses*
>
> *Two small pieces of plastic wrap*
>
> *An 8″ (20 cm) long piece of floral wire*
>
> *Green floral tape*
>
> *Green tissue paper scraps*
>
> *Scissors*

TWIST TIE

1. Pleat only the middle of each dollar bill, up and down like a fan.

2. Place the pleated sections of the bills next to each other and tie them together with the twist tie.

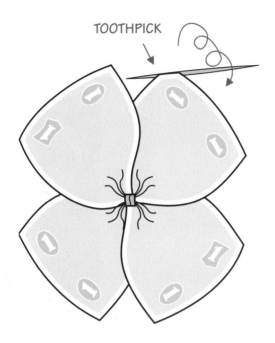

TOOTHPICK

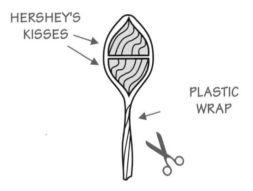

HERSHEY'S KISSES

PLASTIC WRAP

3a. Spread the four ends of the bills evenly and form a bowl shape.

3b. Roll the eight corners of the bills diagonally over the toothpick.

4. Place the flat ends of two Hershey's Kisses together. Wrap them in plastic wrap and twist it underneath. Cut off excess plastic wrap 1" (2 cm) below the Kisses.

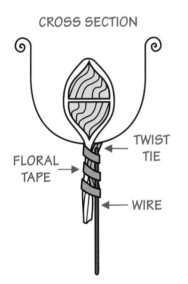

CROSS SECTION

FLORAL TAPE

TWIST TIE

WIRE

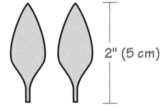

2" (5 cm)

6a. Cut out two leaves from green tissue paper.

6b. Wrap floral tape along the whole length of the wire, stretching it as you go. Fix in the two leaves.

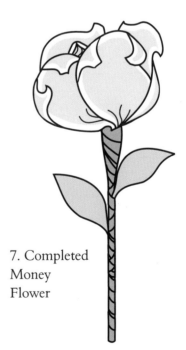

5. Insert the assembled Kisses into the middle of the money flower. Place a piece of wire next to the twist tie. Wrap floral tape tightly around the twist tie, plastic wrap, and wire.

7. Completed Money Flower

Optional

You can glue on small pieces of tape to keep the edges of the bills from gaping.

◤ PICTURE FRAME

Family photos turn into inexpensive gifts when placed in origami frames. Choose black construction paper or gift wrap with small patterns, whatever complements the subjects of your photos best.

You need:

> *A square of paper, with 8″ (20 cm) sides. This will fit a 6″ x 4″ (15 cm x 10 cm) photo trimmed to a 4″ (10 cm) square. For any other photo sizes, make the sides of the square twice as long as the photo you plan to frame.*

If the paper is colored on only one side, begin with the colored side facing up.

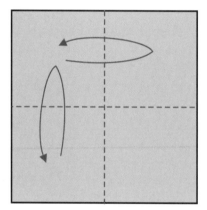

1a. Fold the square in half in both directions.

1b. Unfold it both time.

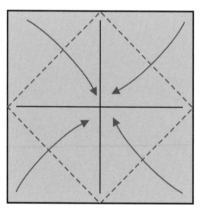

2. Fold the four corners to the center.

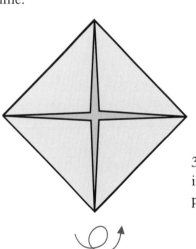

3. In origami language this shape is called a Blintz base. Turn the paper over from front to back.

36

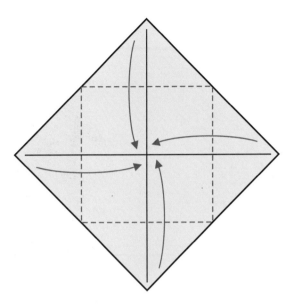

4. Fold the four corners to the center again.

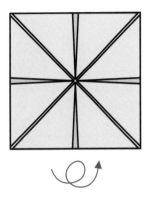

5. Turn the paper over.

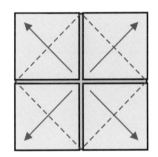

6. Fold the corners from the center to the outside.

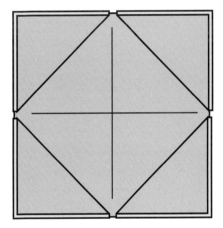

7. Completed Picture Frame

How to Insert the Picture

Trim the photograph as necessary. Check that the area you want to display fits into the available space. Open the frame temporarily to insert the photo without having to bend it.

Photo Stand

If the paper you have used is quite stiff, the bottom flap at the back of the frame can be pulled away to make the photo stand up.

◣ TORAH SCROLL

For unusual Hanukkah decorations, attach Torah Scrolls to gift wrap or set them on the dinner table.

You need:

A paper square

If paper is colored on only one side, begin with the colored side up.

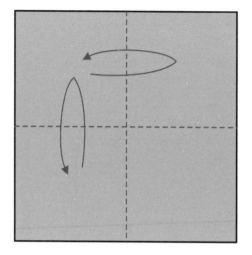

1a. Fold the paper in half both ways.

1b. Unfold it each time.

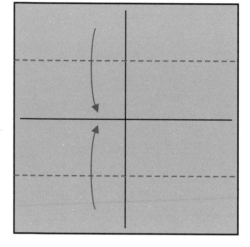

2. Fold two opposite edges to the middle.

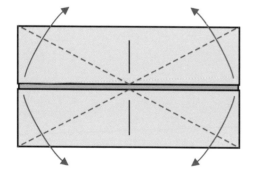

3. Make four creases from the center to the outside corners, as shown.

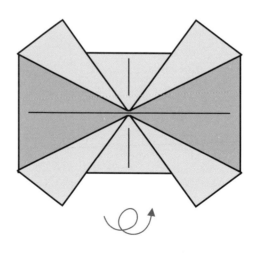

4. Turn the paper over.

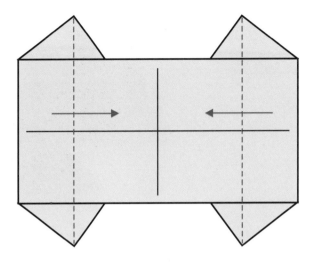

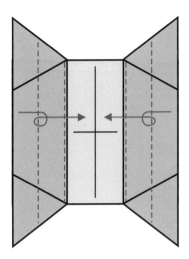

5a. On the left make a crease through the highest and lowest points of the triangles.

5b. Repeat this on the right.

6. Double over the edges twice on the left and twice on the right.

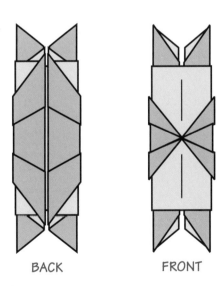

BACK   FRONT

7. Completed Torah Scroll

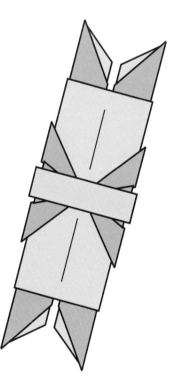

Optional

Cut a narrow strip of paper and wind it around the middle of the scroll. Tape or glue the strip together at the back.

CHRISTMAS STOCKINGS

You can make Christmas Stockings as tree ornaments or earrings, for yourself or as gifts.

You need:

A piece of paper 4″ x 5 ½″ (10 cm x 15 cm)

Gold thread or ornament wire hook

If paper is colored on only one side, begin with the white side of the paper facing up.

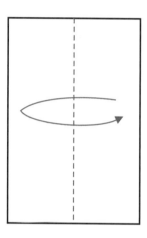

1. Fold the paper in half lengthwise. Unfold it.

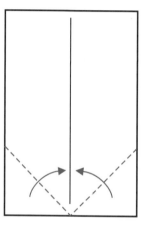

2. Fold the bottom corners to the middle, as shown.

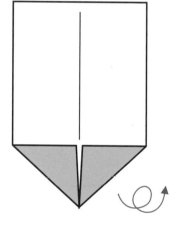

3. Turn the paper over.

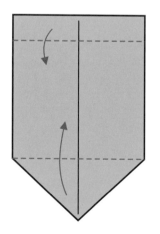

4a. Fold the top edge over for the white cuff.

4b. Fold up the bottom corner.

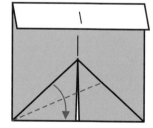

5. You have a triangle on the front. Fold the left slanted edge to the bottom edge.

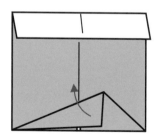

6. Unfold it.

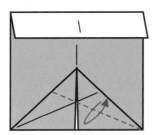

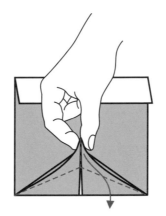

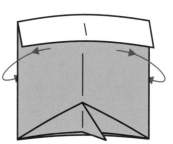

7. Repeat Steps 5 and 6 on the right.

8. Pinch the top of the triangle between your thumb and forefinger and push down to meet the creases you just made. See the next drawing.

9. Roll the sides of the paper to the back.

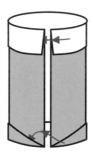

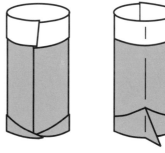

BACK   FRONT

10. Overlap the edges by sliding the top and the bottom under the overlaps on the opposite side. If you like, you can hold the cuff together with a dab of glue.

11. Completed Christmas Stocking

Ornaments

Christmas Stockings look more impressive when they are paired. Loop two together by piercing a hole on the left side of one stocking and on the right side of the other.

Earrings

For a pair of earrings fold two pieces of red origami paper 2" x 3" (5 cm x 8 cm) into Christmas Stockings. Pierce a hole on the left side of one earring and on the right side of the other. For pierced ears attach earring wires. For non-pierced ears attach loops of thread to hang around each ear.

◣ GIFT ENVELOPE

Here is the perfect wrapping for flat gifts or money. The gift envelope can be made from gift wrap or wallpaper. Wallpaper is not suitable for most origami, but in this case it works well because the folding is not too detailed. Wall-covering materials made of paper and with the least amount of plastic hold creases best. Home supply stores will often give away sample books for free.

You need:

A piece of gift wrap, 12″ x 20″ (30 cm x 50 cm)

Begin with the white side of the paper facing up.

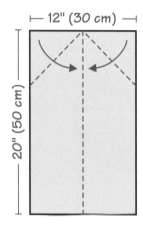

1a. Fold the paper in half the long way.

1b. Unfold it.

1c. Fold two corners to the middle line you just creased.

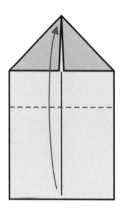

2. Fold the bottom edge up to the top corner.

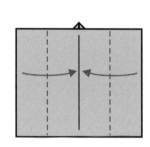

3. Fold the outer edges to the middle.

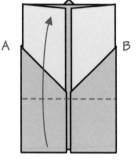

4. Fold the bottom edge to corners A and B.

5. Tuck the top flap behind one layer of the front pocket.

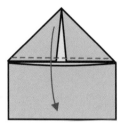

6. Fold the upper part over.

Other Sizes

You can make the envelope smaller or larger to fit the size of your gift, by increasing or decreasing the size of the piece of paper.

No-Sew Fabric Purse

Make the envelope from fabric instead of paper. It's a great way to match a purse to any outfit.

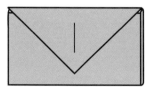

7. Completed Gift Envelope

◤ CANDLE

Candles can be used in Christmas, Hanukkah, and Kwanzaa celebrations.

You need:

A piece of paper 1 ½″ x 6″ (3 cm x 15 cm)

If the paper is colored on only one side, begin with the white side facing up.

1a. Fold the strip in half. Unfold it.

1b. Fold the top corners to the middle.

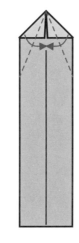

2. Fold the slanted edges to the middle.

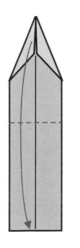

3. Fold the pointed corner to the bottom edge.

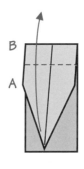

4. Fold up the pointed corner. Note that A ends up on B.

5. Fold in the corners at the bottom of the pleat. Note that they do not reach all the way to the middle.

6. Unfold the same corners and tuck them in between the two layers of paper (reverse folds).

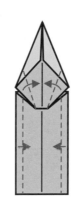

7a. Fold the slanted edges toward the middle, grasping only one flap.

7b. Fold the straight outside edges in about ¼″ (½″ cm).

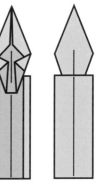

BACK   FRONT

8. Completed Candle

KINARA CANDLE HOLDER

The Kinara Candle Holder is central to the Kwanzaa celebration and symbolizes African ancestors. On the first night usually the black candle is lighted in the spirit of *umoja* or unity. One more candle is added each subsequent night of the seven-day celebration.

You need:

> *A strip of heavy gold foil paper, 12″ x 3″ (30 cm x 7 ½ cm) (if necessary use regular weight gold foil gift wrap doubled)*

Begin with the colored side of paper facing up.

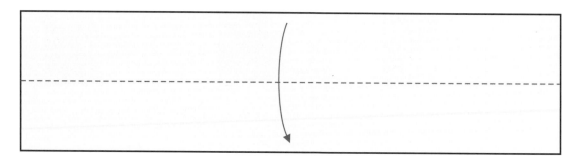

1. Fold strip in half lengthwise.

FOLDED EDGE

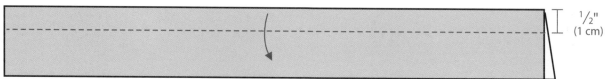

½"
(1 cm)

2. Fold folded edge down ½ (1 cm).

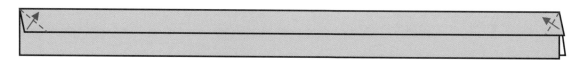

3. Fold the two outside corners up to the folded edge, as shown.

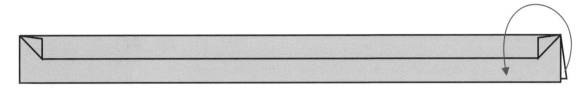

4. Swing the back layer of paper over to the front.

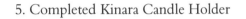

5. Completed Kinara Candle Holder

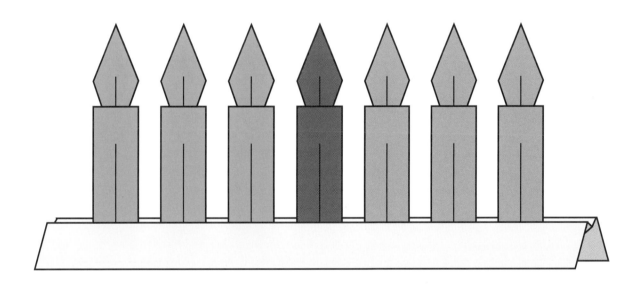

Assembling the Kinara Candle Holder

Make three red, one black, and three green origami candles (see previous project). Insert them into the long slit. If they tilt forward, cut $1/8$" off the long edge on the back layer of the Candle Holder.

Menorah

For Hanukkah, make a Candle Holder but insert nine origami candles. On the first night insert a candle in the middle and one at the end. On each of the seven subsequent nights add one more candle.

SIX-POINTED STAR

A Six-Pointed Star is always a popular decoration, but is also the well-known symbol of the Jewish religion, usually called the Star of David. You can fold it to decorate greeting cards and gift packages or to make earrings.

The large shaded triangle shown on the next page helps you prepare the triangular pieces of paper which you need for folding the star. Trace or photocopy the triangle and cut it out. Then use it as a template to cut out your own triangle. Each corner contains a 60-degree angle. You can choose blue paper, which is the Israeli national color, or other colors.

You need:

> *Foil gift wrap or other paper*
>
> *A pencil*
>
> *A ruler*
>
> *Scissors*

If the paper is colored on only one side, begin with the white side facing up.

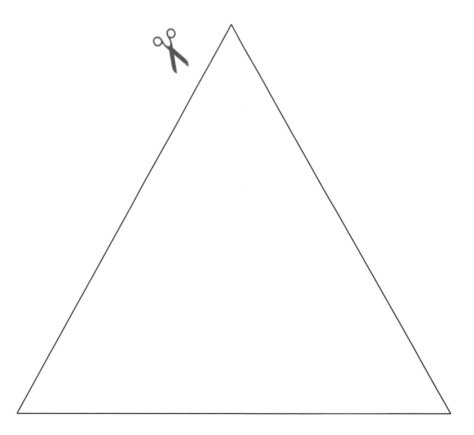

1. Trace or photocopy the large equilateral triangle onto your paper and cut it out.

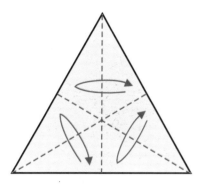 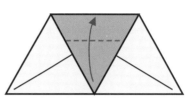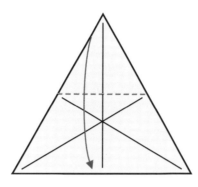

2. Fold the triangle in half, right through the middle of one corner. Unfold it and repeat with the other two corners.

3. Fold the top corner to the bottom edge.

4. Fold it up again, making the crease where all the lines cross in the middle of the paper.

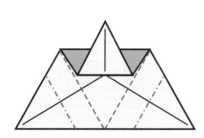 

5. Repeat Steps 2 and 3 with the other two corners.

6. Slip the corner of triangle A under triangle B. This locks the paper and prevents it from unfolding.

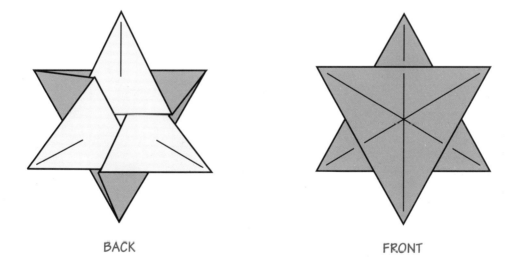

BACK

FRONT

7. Completed Six-Pointed Star

◤ TURKEY

The body of the Turkey is made from a square of plain colored paper. The tail is pleated from a long strip of colorful gift wrap. This can be a wonderful table decoration for your holiday meals.

You need:

> **A 6″ (15 cm) square for the Turkey**
>
> **A strip of gift wrap, 3½″ x 15″ (9 cm x 35 cm) for the tail**
>
> **Scissors**
>
> **A stapler**

If the paper is colored on only one side, begin with the white side facing up.

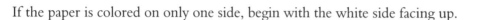

1a. Fold the square corner to corner.

1b. Unfold it.

2. Fold the outer edges to the crease you just made.

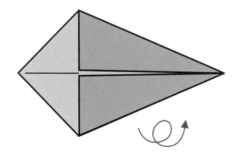

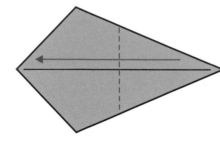

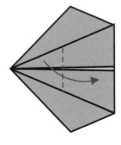

3. Turn the paper over.

4. Fold the paper in half.

5. Fold the corner to the base line for the head.

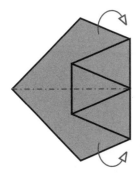 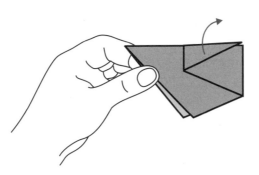 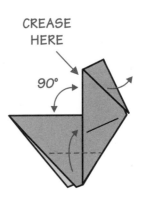

6. Mountain fold the paper in half the long way. The head and neck will be on the outside.

7. Hold the body loosely with one hand. With the other hand, pull the neck up. Crease the front edge to keep the neck up.

8a. Pull the head out and make a crease at the back of the head.

8b. Fold the bottom corner up, first on the front, then on the back.

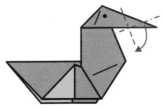 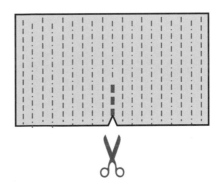

9a. Twist the front of the head so that it points to the body and looks like the wattle. Tuck the tip in between the two layers of the neck.

9b. Bring the two bottom corners to the outside to make the Turkey stand.

10a. Pleat the strip of paper back and forth like a fan.

10b. Cut a short slit in the middle of the fan.

10c. Staple the fan to the turkey with half the fan on each side of the body. Spread the top of the fan.

11. Completed Turkey

◣ DOVE CANDY DISH

The dove symbolizes the message of peace, which pervades the holiday season. The Biblical story about Noah's Ark relates that, after forty days of flooding, the dove brought the good news that the water was receding and land was reappearing.

You need:

A paper square

An 8″ (20 cm) square results in a 5″ (13 cm) candy dish.

If the paper is colored on only one side, begin with the colored side facing up.

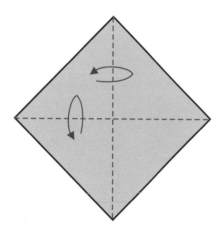

1a. Fold the square from corner to corner in both directions.

1b. Unfold it each time.

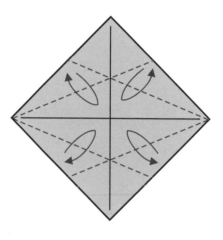

2. Fold all four edges to one of the creases in turn, unfolding the paper each time.

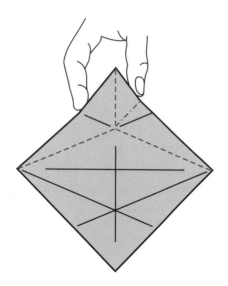

3a. Pinch the upper corner between your thumb and forefinger and guide the paper so that it meets the two creases made in Step 2.

3b. Bend the corner, which is still between your fingers, to the right.

3c. Repeat Steps 3a and 3b with the lower corner.

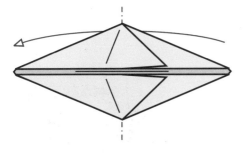

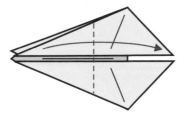

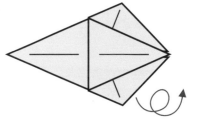

4. Mountain fold the right side under. See the next drawing.

5. In origami language this shape is called a Fish base. With the front flap only, fold the left corner over to the right.

6. Turn the paper over.

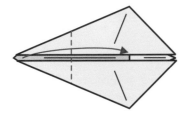

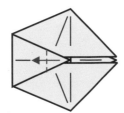

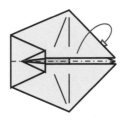

7. Fold the left corner over. Note that the tip ends up where the hidden layer of paper peeks across.

8. Fold the tip over.

9. Mountain fold the paper in half, to the back.

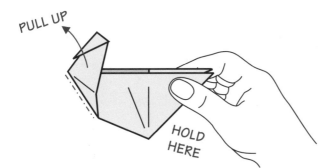

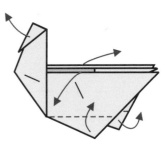

10. Hold the paper with one hand. With the other hand, pull up the neck. To make it stay in place, crease the short, slanted edge at the bottom.

11a. Pull the head forward and press it flat at the back to make it stay in place.

11b. Fold the bottom corners to the outside to make a stand for the candy dish.

11c. Open the wings wide to make room for candy.

12. Completed Dove Candy Dish

SANTA CLAUS

Origami Santas make great tree ornaments, gift wrap attachments, and greeting cards.

You need:

A paper square, red on one side and white on the other

Begin with the red side facing up.

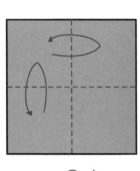

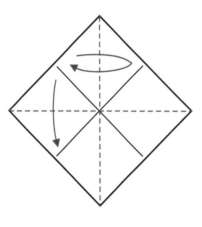

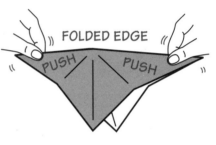

1a. Fold the square in half, both ways. Unfold the paper so that it lies flat each time.

1b. Turn the paper over.

2a. Fold the paper from corner to corner and unfold it.

2b. Fold the paper from corner to corner in the other direction and leave it folded. You will have a triangle.

3. Grasp the paper with both hands at the folded edge in the exact positions shown in the drawing. Move your hands toward each other until the paper is formed into a smaller triangle. Place it flat on the table.

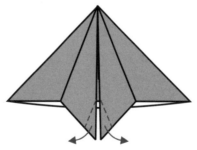

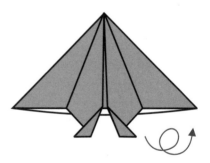

4a. Make sure the triangle has two flaps on each side. If you have only one flap on one side and three flaps on the other, flip one flap over.

4b. Fold the outside edges to the middle, on the front only.

5. Fold the bottom corners to the outside to form Santa's feet.

6. Turn the paper over.

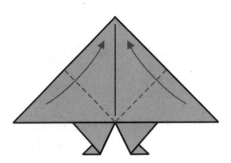

7. Fold the outside corners to the top corner.

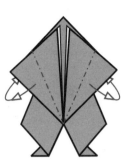

8. Mountain fold the side edges under.

9. Open the two flaps to the outside.

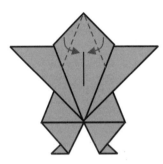

10. Fold the two edges at the top to the middle, to make Santa's hat.

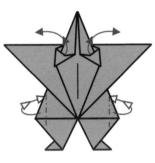

11a. Complete the hat by poking into the "pockets" and pushing them to the outside. In origami language this is called a squash fold. See the next drawing for the result.

11b. Narrow the sides of Santa's coat by mountain folding the corners to the back.

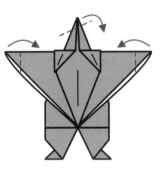

12a. Twist the top of Santa's hat into a tassel.

12b. Make white fur trim at the ends of both arms: Poke in between the layers of each arm and fold back the corner.

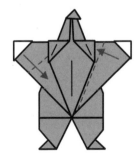

13. On the left, fold one arm down. On the right, fold the other arm up.

14. Completed Santa Claus

Ho Ho Ho

You can draw on eyes and glue on a white cotton beard and a tassel.

◣ KWANZAA BOWL

Filling bowls with small personal gifts is a popular custom in most Kwanzaa celebrations. Handmade gifts are especially welcome because they symbolize the fruits of labor. Given this theme, it is very appropriate to craft the bowl from paper. Family members and friends can be asked to fill them with other origami, drawings, or poems about Kwanzaa.

Gift wrap and art papers work well for this bowl. Before folding a full size bowl, it's a good idea to practice with a smaller piece of paper.

You need:

A paper square, with 20″ (50 cm) sides

If the paper is colored on only one side, begin with the white side facing up.

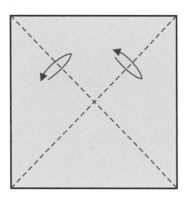

1. Fold the square from corner to corner in both directions. Unfold it both times.

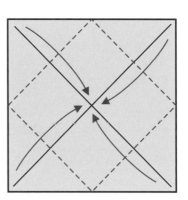

2. Fold all four corners to the center.

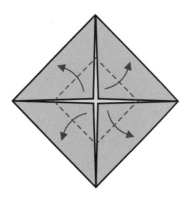

3. In origami language this shape is called a Blintz base. Fold the four corners from the center out to the edges.

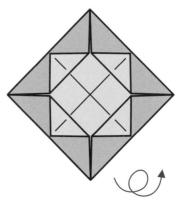

4. Turn the paper over.

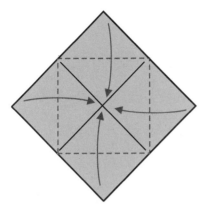

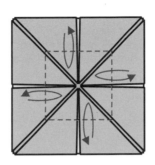

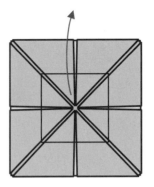

5. Fold all four corners to the center again.

6. Fold the four edges to the middle. Unfold them each time.

7. Lift up one triangular flap.

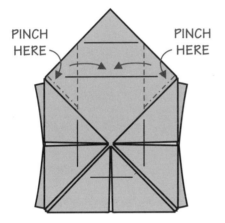

PINCH HERE

PINCH HERE

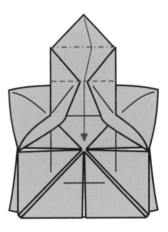

8a. Valley fold the right corner and push it over to the middle, but leave the outside layer of paper alone. A mountain fold forms on the diagonal crease, and the paper rises up.

8b. Now fold the left corner over to the middle in the same way. These two folds leave the flap raised.

9a. Bring the flap down, locking in both corners. The sides of the bowl will begin to form.

9b. Repeat Steps 8 and 9a at the opposite end.

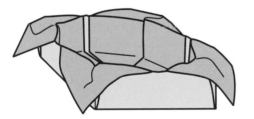

10. Shape the bowl by curving the outside petals. Make the square box rounder by softening the four corners.

11. Completed Kwanzaa Bowl

Sizes

A 20" (50 cm) paper square results in a 7" (18 cm) bowl. For folding smaller 4" (10 cm) candy dishes, begin with a 10" (25 cm) square.

◣ STAR OF BETHLEHEM

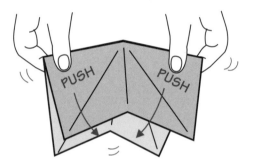

Most origami stars have rays of equal lengths, but I have designed a star with two long and two short rays, to resemble the more traditional depiction of the Star of Bethlehem. You can combine this star with The Three Kings to make a Christmas scene.

You need:

A square of foil paper

A 6″ (15 cm) square produces a 6″ (15 cm) star

If paper is colored on only one side, begin with the white side facing up.

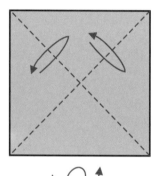

1a. Fold the square from corner to corner in both directions. Unfold the paper so that it lies flat each time.

1b. Turn the paper over.

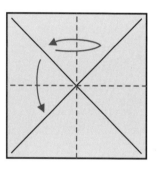

2a. Fold the paper in half and unfold it.

2b. Fold the paper in half the other way and leave it folded.

3. Grasp the paper with both hands at the folded edge in the exact positions shown in the drawing. Move your hands toward each other until the paper is formed into a square. Place it flat on the table.

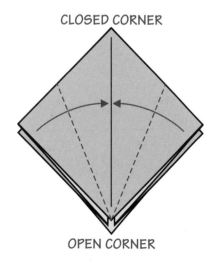

CLOSED CORNER

OPEN CORNER

4a. Make sure the square has two flaps on each side. If you have only one flap on one side and three flaps on the other, flip one flap over. In origami language this is called the Preliminary or Square base.

4b. Place the square with the closed corner away from you. Fold the outer edges of the front flaps to the middle crease.

4c. Turn the paper over and repeat Step 4b with the two flaps on the back.

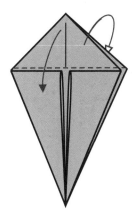

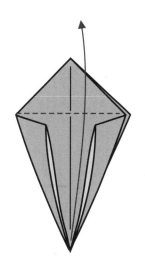

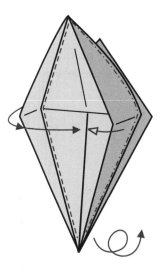

5. Fold the triangle at the top forward and back, bringing it back to its original position. This makes a helpful crease for the next step.

6. Open the front flap slightly. This exposes the corner of the paper. Lift it up in the direction of the arrow and make a valley fold on the helpful crease you made in Step 5.

7a. The outer edges of the paper will move to the middle as you proceed and will form a diamond shape.

7b. Turn the paper over and repeat Steps 6 and 7a on the back.

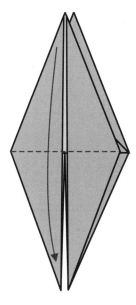

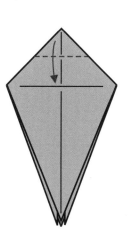

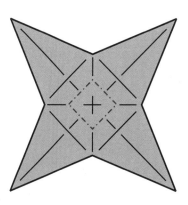

8. In origami language this shape is called the Bird base.

8a. Fold the front flap down.

8b. Repeat Step 8a on the back.

9. Fold the top corner down to the crease on the front and unfold it. Fold the same corner to the crease on the back and unfold it again.

10a. Let the paper open up, and mountain fold the four crease lines that form the small square in the middle.

10b. Then, fold the paper into the previous shape again, but with top corner hidden inside. See the next drawing. This move is called a sink fold.

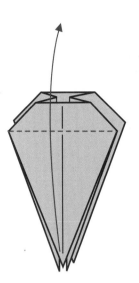

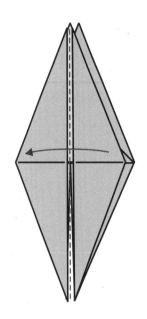

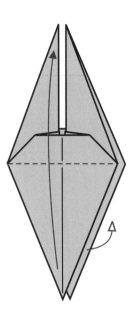

11. Lift up the front and back flaps.

12a. Fold the right flap to left, as if turning the page of a book.

12b. Turn the paper over and repeat Step 12a on the back, again folding from right to left.

13. Fold up the front and back flaps.

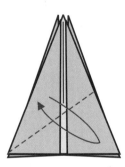

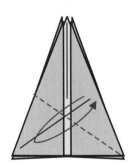

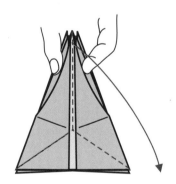

14. Make a rabbit's ear with the front flap by following these moves:

Fold the left edge to the bottom edge. Unfold it.

15. Fold the right edge to the bottom edge. Unfold it.

16a. Pinch the top corner between your thumb and forefinger and guide it to the right. See next drawing.

16b. Repeat the rabbit's ear on the back flap.

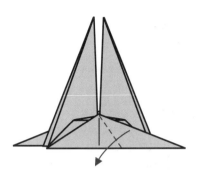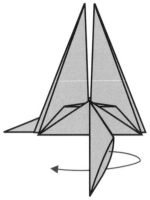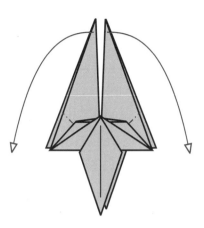

17. Fold over the long edge of the rabbit's ear to the middle on the front.

18a. Poke in between the two layers of the rabbit's ear and push the underside over to the left. Flatten it to look like the next drawing.

18b. Repeat Steps 17 and 18a on the back. In origami language this is called a squash fold.

19a. Reverse fold both long points. First fold them straight out to the sides.

19b. Fold both points up again.

19c. Fold them out to the sides again, but this time reverse the central crease into a valley fold and guide the paper to lie in between the main layers of paper.

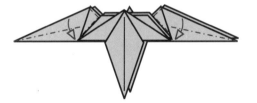

20. Narrow the long edges of both rays, by bringing the top edges to the horizontal lower edges. Start at the narrow point and tuck in the extra at the other end, first on the front, then on the back.

21. Spread the four long rays and four short rays evenly.

22. Completed Star of Bethlehem

◤ REINDEER

You will find many uses for these reindeer once you know how to fold them. They can stand up as table or mantel decorations or they can be glued on greeting cards and posters.

You need:

> *A 10" (25 cm) paper square*
>
> *Two 3 ½" x ½" (8 cm x 1 cm) paper strips*
>
> *Scissors*

If paper is colored on only one side, begin with the colored side of the paper facing up.

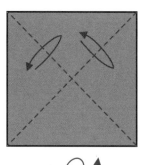

1a. Fold the square from corner to corner in both directions. Unfold the paper so that it lies flat each time.

1b. Turn the paper over.

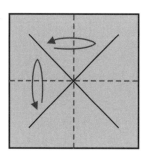

2a. Fold the paper in half and unfold it.

2b. Fold the paper in half the other way and leave it folded.

3. Grasp the paper with both hands at the folded edge in the exact positions shown in the drawing. Move your hands toward each other until the paper is formed into a square. Place it flat on the table.

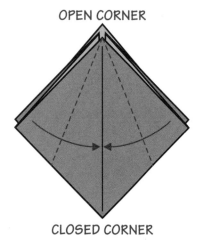

OPEN CORNER

CLOSED CORNER

4a. Make sure the square has two flaps on each side. If you have only one flap on one side and three flaps on the other, flip one flap over. In origami language this shape is called the Preliminary or Square base.

4b. Place the square with the open corner away from you. Fold the outer edges of the front flaps to the middle crease. Note that the creases begin at the open corner.

4c. Turn the paper over and repeat Step 4b with the two flaps on the back.

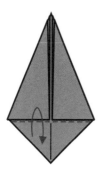

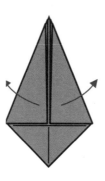

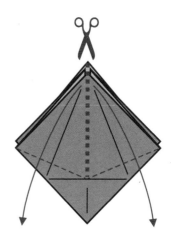

5. Fold the triangle at the bottom forward and back, ending up in its original position.

6. Flip the two front flaps out to the sides. Repeat on the back.

7a. Cut the front and back flaps in half, down to the triangle.

7b. Fold down the top corners as far as you can on the front and on the back.

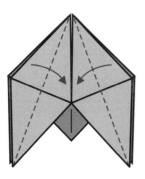

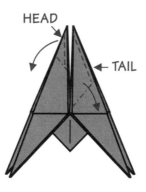

8. Fold the sides to the middle, first on the front and then on the back.

9. Reverse fold the head and tail by swinging them down in between the main layers of paper.

10. This shows Step 9 completed.

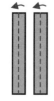

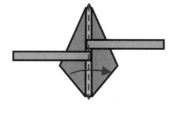

11. Make the antlers by folding the two strips of paper in half lengthwise.

12a. Spread the head apart.

12b. Tuck the ends of the antlers inside the pockets, one to the right and the other to the left.

12c. Fold up the head again.

13a. Reverse fold the nose under.

13b. Zigzag fold both antlers.

14. Completed Reindeer

ACKNOWLEDGEMENTS

I owe a debt of gratitude to many friends in the international origami community who, over many years, have always been ready to share their interest in origami. I wish I could name everyone, but regret that is impossible. I would like to thank those who have patiently participated in the time-consuming task of testing the directions: Heather and Julia Anderson, John Andrisan, Jackie Booth, Sharon Brengel, Jim Cowling, V'Ann Cornelius, Charles de Stefano, Ed Epps, Steve Hecht, Judy Jaskowiak, Cath Kachur, Zoe Lehman, Dane Petersen, Nancy Petersen, Lisa and Mark Saliers, Yvonne Perez-Collins, Arlene Pollock, Shoshana Resnikoff, David and Michael Sanchez, Arnold Tubis, members of Origami San Diego, and, of course, my grandchildren, Tyler and Yolanda Anyon; Erin Hook; Dennis and Janet Temko; David, Perri, and Rachel Temko.